A souvenir guide

Coughton Court

Warwickshire

National Trust

A Dearly Loved Home

Set in the once great Forest of Arden, Coughton Court has been our family home for six centuries – an astonishing fact, when you consider that most families move house every five years or so.

At a time when we are as a nation so interested in knowing more about our ancestors and where we came from, we are fortunate enough to know a great deal about our family. We can trace our roots back to Charlemagne (*c.*800AD) and we know that in 1409 the Throckmorton family came to Coughton, through the marriage of Eleanor de Spiney and Sir John de Throckmorton.

Walking around the house and gardens today, it is hard to imagine that there were times when it would have been dangerous to be a Throckmorton; times when followers of Catholicism became outsiders in their own country. Echoes from this period of England's history resonate still today – even now a Catholic cannot be heir to the throne. Around the house you will find all manner of family treasures that have connections with these dark and dangerous times, and you will see rooms and hiding places which link Coughton with the fallout from the Reformation and the Gunpowder Plot of 1605.

More than four centuries later, Coughton has now entered one of the most tranquil periods in its history. The gardens that my daughter, Christina Williams, and I have created are a colourful celebration of this. I hope that you will appreciate our family home quite simply for the beauty of its architecture and its fascinating collections of historic furniture and

artefacts; but that you will also be intrigued and moved by the stories of my ancestors. It is still very much our home and we are delighted, together with the National Trust, to be able to share it with you.

Clare McLaren-Throckmorton

Opposite Gumboots in the Garden Hall

Right Mrs Clare McLaren-Throckmorton in the Blue Drawing Room in 1996; painted by Sergei Pavlenko

One Family's Journey from Danger to Triumph

Twenty generations of the Throckmorton family have lived at Coughton (pronounced 'coat-on') since 1409, when they inherited part of the estate by marriage. They live here still, but over the past six centuries they have faced many challenges.

Loyal to the old faith: Danger

Following the Protestant Reformation of the 1530s, most of the Throckmortons remained faithful to the old Catholic religion. During the reign of Elizabeth I, they were persecuted as *recusants* (from the Latin *recusare*, 'to refuse') for refusing to accept the new Protestant faith. They suffered fines, imprisonment and even execution. In the 17th century, the house was ransacked not once, but twice – by Parliamentary soldiers in 1644, and by a Protestant mob in 1688.

To practise their religion openly, the Throckmortons had to travel to the Continent. During the 18th century, they were still forbidden from holding public office. They led the campaign to remove these restrictions, and in 1831 Sir Robert Throckmorton, 8th Bt became one of the first Catholic MPs to take a seat in the House of Commons. The Throckmortons of Coughton Court remain Catholics to this day.

Not forgotten: Triumph

Throughout these ordeals, the Throckmortons retained Coughton. At the same time, by judicious marriages they acquired substantial estates in Buckinghamshire, Oxfordshire, Worcestershire, Berkshire and Devon. These marriages also brought with them Catholic treasures. For long periods, they preferred to live away from Coughton, but they preserved their ancestral Warwickshire home and chose the nearby church as their final resting place.

Above Celebration: The Dining Room table laid for supper

Left Danger: During the years of persecution, the Throckmortons held secret services in the Tower Room

Key people

Sir George Throckmorton (*c*.1489–1553) completes the gatehouse.

The brothers **Sir Robert** (d.1580) and **Sir Nicholas Throckmorton** (1515-71) choose different faiths.

Sir Robert Throckmorton, 4th Bt (1702–91) builds Buckland House as his principal home, but cherishes Coughton.

Sir John Throckmorton, 5th Bt (1753–1819), leading member of the Cisalpine Club, which argued that Catholicism was perfectly compatible with being a loyal subject of the Crown.

Lilian, Lady Throckmorton (d.1955) keeps Coughton going against the odds while her young son is growing up. She arranges for the house to be handed over to the National Trust.

Key dates

1409	John Throckmorton marries Eleanor de Spiney, heiress to part of the Coughton estate.
***c*.1510–30s**	Sir Robert Throckmorton and his son Sir George build the gatehouse.
1530s	Henry VIII introduces the Reformation to England.
1605	Gunpowder Plot to assassinate James I by blowing up Parliament. The conspirators include several relations of the Throckmortons. Coughton Court rented by one of the Plotters, Sir Everard Digby.
1643-4	During the Civil War, the house is occupied by Parliamentary soldiers and badly damaged.
1660s	House repaired.
1688	Protestant mob sets alight the Catholic chapel in the east wing.
1780s	Sir Robert Throckmorton, 4th Bt remodels the house in the Gothick style.
1829	Catholic Emancipation Act lifts final restrictions on Catholics.
1851	Work starts on building Catholic church at the end of the south drive.
1946	Coughton acquired by the National Trust.
1992	Christina Williams designs the new scheme in the Walled Garden.

When the 4th Baronet decided to modernise Coughton in the 1780s, he did so with remarkable sympathy for the old fabric. When money became short in the late 19th and 20th centuries, the Throckmortons sold off most of the estates they had inherited by marriage and returned to Coughton. They brought with them paintings, furniture, ceramics, embroideries and books, which today are displayed at Coughton for all to enjoy.

Exploring the House

The Gatehouse

Tall, battlemented gatehouses had been a feature of medieval castles for centuries. They remained popular as dramatic statements of authority in the Tudor period, long after they had lost their original defensive purpose. The Coughton gatehouse would originally have looked even more impressive when reflected in the moat that once surrounded the house.

The West Front

The Warwickshire antiquary William Dugdale believed that Sir George had intended to make the rest of Coughton match his grand stone gatehouse, but for the next two and a half centuries the wings flanking the gatehouse seem to have remained an asymmetrical muddle.

In the 1780s the 4th Baronet imposed a little order by inserting balancing trios of pointed windows on the first floor to match the pretty Dutch gables put up during the late 17th-century restoration. A coat of whitewash unified the whole. In the 1820s the gables were taken down, and the roof hidden behind a castellated parapet. At the same time the walls were rendered with cement coloured to resemble stone.

The Courtyard

Originally, the gatehouse formed the grand entrance to an enclosed courtyard, much like the quadrangle of a traditional Oxbridge college. The east wing was ransacked and burned in 1688 and eventually demolished by the 4th Baronet in the 1780s, leaving one side open to the countryside beyond.

The North Wing

This range (on the left, looking from the gatehouse) seems to have originally comprised lodgings for visitors. It was at first

Building the Gatehouse

Stage 1: The earliest part is the central bay of the ground floor. This contains the arched gateway, which was originally open to let horses and carts pass through into the central courtyard. It probably dates from the time of Sir Robert Throckmorton, who died on crusade in 1519.

Stage 2: Sir Robert's son, Sir George Throckmorton, appears to have completed the upper storeys, which were constructed from a slightly different stone, in the 1530s. (Curiously, however, the gatehouse was not mentioned by the antiquary John Leland, who passed this way during his travels of 1535–43. So it may be rather later.) Octagonal, castellated turrets flank double-height bay windows. We do not know the name of Coughton's architect, but whoever designed the gatehouse produced one of the grandest and most sophisticated examples of early Tudor architecture.

In deference to his monarch, Sir George placed Henry VIII's coat of arms below the second-floor bay window. His own Throckmorton arms appear below the first-floor window. The bottom half of the family coat of arms fell to the ground on the very day in 1916 that the heir to the estate, Lt-Col. Courtenay Throckmorton, was killed in action in Iraq. It has never been replaced.

Stage 3: The third element of the gatehouse comprises the flanking stone bays. These look convincingly Tudor, but in fact did not assume their present form until the 1780s, when the 4th Baronet created a new staircase in the southern block to improve circulation between the main floors. Such restraint in remodelling an ancient building was very rare in the 18th century.

only a single storey, and was extended to its present height in the late 16th century. The ground floor was rebuilt in brick after the Civil War devastation of Coughton. This wing is now the family's private quarters.

The South Wing

This probably always contained the principal reception rooms, including a great hall (now the Saloon), which rose the full height of the building at the east end. The smoke-blackened roof timbers remain in the loft space. In the 1660s the great hall was divided horizontally to create a suite of fine rooms on the first floor, which were lit by large windows. In the Elizabethan era this wing was widened on the courtyard side to allow for a passageway so that the gatehouse now stands asymmetrically between the two surviving wings. Later, a further block of family rooms including a new parlour and dining room was added at the south-west corner, topped by Dutch gables, which still survive. At the same time a Perpendicular stone doorway was rescued from the rubble of the demolished east wing and reused here to provide a suitably impressive entrance to the Saloon.

Above **The North Wing**

Opposite top **The West Front in the early 19th century**

Opposite below **The Gatehouse**

The Front Hall

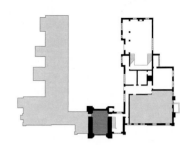

Above The Front Hall

This originally served as the gatehouse passageway and was open at both ends. In the 1780s the 4th Baronet turned it into a room decorated in the Gothick style. The ceiling was given a fine fan vault and the walls lined out to resemble masonry, although the whole effect was in fact created from plaster

Right The hat-stand displays Mrs McLaren-Throckmorton's love of travel. She brings a new hat home each time she goes away!

Below The fan-vaulted ceiling is made from plaster painted to resemble stone

rather than stone. The western opening was walled up, leaving only a narrow door flanked by arched windows, which, in keeping with the medieval mood, were filled with old heraldic glass commemorating the Throckmortons and their relations. The glass was moved to the Blue Drawing Room in 1835, when the 7th Baronet turned the space back into a carriageway and hung the present oak doors. Plain coloured glass now fills their upper lights.

Furniture

The four *mid-Georgian hall chairs* bear the Throckmorton crest and are typical of the hard-wearing, if uncomfortable, furniture found in many country house entrance halls.

The *longcase clock* rings both the Westminster and Whittington chimes. It was a 21st birthday present to Sir Robert Throckmorton, 11th Bt.

The *umbrella stand* is decorated with the Stapleton and Acton arms. Members of those families married the 6th and 8th Baronets.

Stone carving

The heraldic cartouche of *c.*1700 bears the Throckmorton and Yate arms. Sir Robert Throckmorton, 3rd Bt, married Mary Yate, heiress to Harvington in Worcestershire and Buckland in Oxfordshire. (Their portraits hang on the stairs.) This stone fragment may come from one of those houses.

Tapestry

The tapestry from the *Rape of the Sabine Women* series was woven in Brussels in the 16th century.

The Staircase

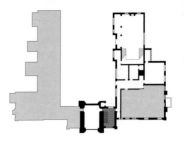

The staircase is the most important and successful of the internal changes the 4th Baronet made to Coughton during his remodelling of the house in the 1780s. Previously, the only link between the main floors on the west side of the house seems to have been the narrow spiral stairs in the corner turrets of the gatehouse. Sir Robert rebuilt the bay immediately to the south of the gatehouse to take an imposing new staircase. It is a subtle marriage of different styles: classical stairs, Tudor windows and Gothick cornice.

To heat this huge space, in 1902 Sir William Throckmorton, 9th Bt installed at the base of the stairs the mammoth *radiator*, of a type more commonly found in churches.

The Throckmorton coat of arms is woven into the modern stair carpet.

Furniture
The *oak table* supports a top decorated in Italy with specimen marbles and the Throckmorton and Acton arms, and so must have been made soon after 1829, when the 8th Baronet married Elizabeth Acton.

Pictures
The walls are painted deep red, a shade traditionally chosen for picture galleries. The room now serves as a vertical portrait gallery of the Throckmortons and their relations. As you climb the stairs, you will encounter

1550s: A family divided
On the bottom flight, the bearded man with a fur collar and black cap resting his hand on a skull (*detail left*) is *Sir Robert Throckmorton* (d.1580), who chose to remain a Catholic and so endured religious persecution during Elizabeth I's reign. Next to him hangs a portrait of his brother, *Sir Nicholas* (1515–71), who chose Protestantism (*detail right*). He was arrested for involvement in the Wyatt rebellion against the Catholic Mary I, but survived. Their mother *Katherine* had no fewer than nineteen children and 112 grandchildren.

succeeding generations from the 16th to the early 19th centuries. The present arrangement was devised in the 1950s by the 11th Baronet's second wife, Lady Isabel. *For full details, see the picture lists provided in the rooms.*

On the landing are three-quarter-length portraits of the 4th Baronet's second wife, *Catherine Collingwood* (d.1761), painted by John Vanderbank in 1737; and of his son-in-law, *Thomas Giffard* (1764–1823). Giffard stands next to a classical bust of the goddess Athene in this characteristic Grand Tour portrait from the Rome studio of Pompeo Batoni.

Hanging further up the stairs are portraits of *Sir Francis Throckmorton*, 2nd Bt (1641–80), painted by Gerard Soest in the 1670s, and his wife, *Anne Monson* (d.1728). Sir Francis restored Coughton after the devastation of the Civil War, but fell out with his wife in later life. The same distinctive, but as yet unidentified, artist painted *Sir Robert Throckmorton*, 3rd Bt (1662–1720) and his wife *Mary Yate* (d.1728).

Sculpture

The white marble bust of *Sir John Throckmorton, 5th Bt* (1753–1819) on the next landing was also conceived in Rome, by the Irish sculptor Christopher Hewetson, and finished after Hewetson's death by Christopher Prosperi in 1800.

Right Sir John Throckmorton, 5th Bt; marble bust by Christopher Hewetson and Christopher Prosperi, 1800

Far right The Staircase decorated for Christmas

The Blue Drawing Room

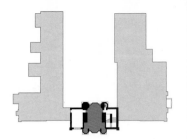

This room occupies the first floor of the original gatehouse, which was probably completed by Sir George Throckmorton in the 1530s. It would have been one of the principal rooms in his house. The two huge oriel windows offer magnificent views over the park in both directions. However, their stone mullions and leaded panes of glass do not offer much protection against the cold. To keep out the draughts, the 7th Baronet blocked up the west window in the 1830s; it was reopened in 1956, when the Tudor stone fireplace was also revealed.

1729: Looking back

Hanging in pride of place over the fireplace is a magnificent portrait of *Sir Robert Throckmorton, 4th Bt* (1702–91), which was painted in France by Nicolas de Largillière in 1729. He wears a ceremonial breastplate (no longer functional armour), a blue velvet jacket embroidered with gold thread by his niece, Sister Frances Wollascott, and a red cloak lined with leopard skin. By the 1720s, Catholics like Sir Robert no longer risked imprisonment or even death for their faith, but they could still be fined and excluded from public office.

Above The Blue Drawing Room

Pictures

Largillière also painted the 4th Baronet's aunt, *Anne Throckmorton* (1664–1734), to the left of the fireplace. She is shown in her wimple as Prioress of the English Augustinian Convent of Notre-Dame-de-Sion in Paris.

On the opposite wall is another portrait by a first-rate French artist: *Lady Mary Herbert* (1659–1744), by François du Troy. Her father, the Catholic 1st Marquess of Powis, had had to flee to France following the overthrow of the Catholic King James II in 1688. Her portrait finds itself here as she was the aunt of the 4th Baronet's first wife.

The 4th Baronet's second wife, *Catherine Collingwood* (d.1761) is depicted in a handsomely framed portrait by George Knapton, who painted many of the leading connoisseurs of the early 18th century.

Catherine herself was a friend of two of the most artistically minded women then living in England, the Duchess of Portland and Mrs Delany.

Knapton also painted the 4th Baronet's eldest son, *George* (1721–67) and George's wife, Anna Maria Paston. George points towards a portrait of a sleeping girl painted in pastel – a technique that Knapton helped to introduce to Britain. George died before his long-lived father, so never owned Coughton, but he brought the ancient Devon estate of Molland into the family by his marriage.

Furniture

The *Boulle clock* bearing the figure of Liberty stands on a kingwood *bureau plat* (desk), c.1760s. The *chandelier* was made in France in the mid-19th century.

The Yellow Drawing Room

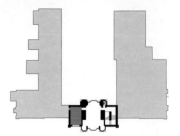

When the 4th Baronet rebuilt the bay next to the gatehouse in the 1780s, this room served as the ante-room to the larger drawing room next door.

Furniture

The *mid-Georgian chairs* have seats which were embroidered in *petit point* in the 1920s by Mrs Langford-Brooke, the great-grandmother of Mrs McLaren-Throckmorton.

The two-tier *chandelier* was made about 1910 by Osler & Faraday, who produced work of the highest quality in their Birmingham factory.

1618: Executed for treason

Hanging above the fireplace is a portrait of Anne Carew. She was the mother of Bess Throckmorton, who had secretly married the courtier and explorer Sir Walter Raleigh in 1591 – much to the fury of Queen Elizabeth, whom she served as a maid of honour. In 1603 Raleigh had been implicated in the Main Plot, in which a group of Catholic conspirators had tried to depose James I. Raleigh was condemned to death and sent to the Tower of London, but was eventually released. However, the disastrous failure of his Guiana expedition led to his execution in 1618.

Right Part of a Worcester dessert service, *c*.1770

Right **Part of a Worcester dessert service, c.1770**

Below **A Coalport service of the 1830s, decorated with maps of the counties of England**

Pictures

The *half-length portrait* was painted in Rome in 1772 by Pompeo Batoni, the most fashionable portraitist in the city. It is inscribed as of the 4th Baronet's eldest grandson, Robert (1750–79), who was making the Grand Tour of Italy at that time. He is shown holding an engraving of the Pantheon, the greatest surviving building of classical antiquity in Rome.

Ceramics

On the wall behind the cabinet hangs part of a first period *Worcester porcelain dessert service* of c.1770, featuring painted urns in superb condition.

On the wall facing the window is a *service of Coalport porcelain plates and dishes, c.1830,* decorated with maps of the counties of England.

The spiral staircase to the Tower Room and roof is narrow and uneven. Please take special care.

The Tower Room
The Roof

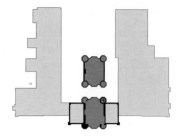

Tabula Eliensis ('Picture of Ely')
This unique painted version of a medieval mural at Ely can be dated to 1596, at the height of the persecution of English Catholics. It depicts, in the centre, Ely Cathedral with its original spire (now gone). Below are the heads of 40 knights and gentlemen, who were quartered at Ely from 1071 to 1076, when they were withdrawn, apparently to the regret of the monks. Also shown are heads of the English monarchs from William Rufus to Elizabeth I. Beneath these are the coats of arms of all the Catholic gentry imprisoned for recusancy in Elizabeth's reign. They are arranged below the places where they were imprisoned.

The Tower Room

The upper rooms of Tudor gatehouses were often reserved for important guests or used as banqueting rooms, where the final course of sweetmeats and other delicacies would be served.

The Tower Room was probably also converted into a makeshift Catholic chapel in Elizabethan times, when the Throckmortons could only celebrate Mass in secret. From here and the rooftop immediately above, they could keep watch over the surrounding countryside and ensure that their worship was not discovered.

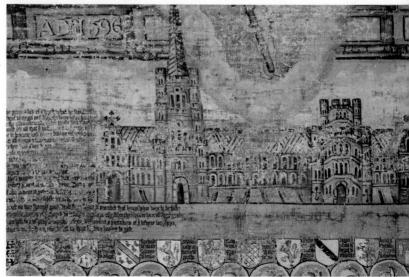

Above **The view south from the roof**

Opposite above **The Tower Room**

Opposite below **The *Picture of Ely* depicts Ely Cathedral and the coats of arms of Catholic gentry in the late 16th century**

Sir William Throckmorton, 9th Bt, discovered the canvas packed away in the attics. It was moved to the Tower Room in 1956, while the roof was being repaired.

The Roof

From the top of the gatehouse you get superb views of the house's complex roofscape and of the surrounding countryside beyond.

1643: A hiding place

If the Throckmortons were interrupted during divine service, their priest could take refuge in the secret chamber they created in the north-east turret in the late 16th century. This 'priest's hole' comprises two compartments – one above another: if the first was discovered by priest-hunters, then the second might be overlooked. It was squeezed below the floor level of the Tower Room and above the spiral staircase, which connected the ground and first floors. When the new staircase was installed in the 1780s, the narrow spiral staircase became redundant, and was sealed up, together with the priest's hole. The upper compartment of the hiding place was rediscovered in 1858, but its lower companion not until 1910, when it was found to contain a straw mattress, a rope ladder, a small piece of tapestry and a folding altar made of leather. These may have been left here in October 1643, when Coughton was occupied by a Parliamentary garrison.

To the west, the avenue of limes (replacing ancient elms lost to disease in the 1970s) adds a focus to the landscape. The avenue frames the gatehouse when looking towards the house from the west. It also leads the eye to the Ridgeway, which runs north–south and over which the Gunpowder Plotters fled as they attempted to escape through the Midlands in the aftermath of the discovery of Guy Fawkes.

To the east there is more variety: the new garden leads the eye from the central courtyard to the River Arrow (a tributary of the Avon) and the gently rolling hills of the ancient Forest of Arden beyond. To the south are Westminster Pool and the family's two places of worship; to the north, the Tudor kitchens and the grand 18th-century stableyard.

Tudor architects loved to build high so that rooftop promenaders could enjoy views like those at Coughton or watch the progress of the hunt. By the early 17th century, buildings such as Lodge Park in Gloucestershire (also in the care of the National Trust) were being erected specifically as grandstands.

The Dining Room

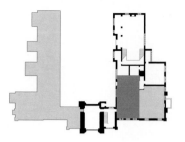

In Elizabethan times, this was probably the great chamber, the principal first-floor reception room, where the Throckmortons would have entertained important guests. It appears to have become the Dining Room in the early 19th century, which cannot have been popular with the household staff, as the kitchen was almost 100 metres away at the opposite corner of the building.

In 1910 the ceiling was raised and decorated in an elaborate neo-Elizabethan style. This was all hidden in 1956, when the ceiling was returned to its earlier height.

Chimneypiece
Pairs of polished slate columns support Ionic capitals and bases of white marble, all apparently mid-17th-century. The oak overmantel was carved with the Throckmorton arms in 1926 by Mr Boot, who was a woodsman on the estate.

Panelling
The frieze features roundels, dragons and human heads in a Renaissance style. The row immediately below is decorated with projecting lozenges flanked by little columns.

Above The carved figures on the panelling are probably mid-16th-century, but were not put up here until 1827, when they were salvaged from Weston Underwood

Left The Dining Room

Above The oak dole-gate came from the convent of Denny, where Elizabeth Throckmorton was the last abbess

The Latin inscription on the hinged central doors can be translated 'May God preserve Dame Elizabeth Throckmorton, Abbess of Denny'. The surviving outer panels are carved with the Sacred Heart, the Tudor rose and the Beaufort portcullis. Elizabeth later lived modestly at Coughton with two of her nuns. The dole-gate was found in a cottage at Ombersley in Worcestershire in 1836.

Furniture

The large rectangular *refectory table*, placed along the wall opposite the fireplace, would have been used for large family gatherings. It is over 5 metres (17 feet) in length and is made from a single piece of oak. Dating back to at least the 1700s, the top is loose, allowing the board to be turned after each use. The *oak buffets* are an early form of side-table used for displaying family silver and for serving food from.

The *wooden goblet* is said to have been made from a mulberry tree under which Shakespeare sat at New Place, Stratford-upon-Avon.

To the left of the fireplace is a *bread box* dating back to before 1637. The inscription is in French and reads 'God Gives All'. Two Throckmorton coats of arms are carved on the front.

Silver

The dining table is laid with *silver candelabra and cruets* inherited from the Acton family.

The *centrepiece* on the refectory table is the Stewards Cup, which was won by the 9th Baronet's horse Herald at Goodwood in 1877.

The rest is plainer. There are panelled doors to match. The upper panels are probably mid-16th-century and are what you would expect to find in an ancient house like Coughton, but, as so often with such wainscotting, they are not quite what they seem. For they appear to have been put up here as late as 1827, having been salvaged from Weston Underwood, the great Throckmorton house in Buckinghamshire, when it was demolished. To add to the air of antiquity, they were stained dark brown and polished, but originally would have been painted.

Dole-gate

On display in this room is an oak dole-gate from the convent of Denny in Cambridge, where Elizabeth Throckmorton was the last abbess in 1539, when the convent was dissolved by Henry VIII. It would have been positioned in the main gate of the convent. Charitable donations of bread would be handed out to the poor through the lower opening (hence the expression 'on the dole').

1831: Celebrating freedom

In May 1831 Sir Robert Throckmorton, 8th Bt, celebrated a momentous turning-point in British history. The Catholic Relief Act had been passed two years earlier, and now he was one of the first Catholic MPs to represent an English constituency since the Reformation.

The Ante-Room
The Tapestry Bedroom

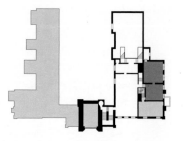

The Ante-Room

The Ante-Room and Tapestry Bedroom form part of the block added to the south-west corner of the house in the late 17th century. This room was reinstated in 1975 by removing earlier partitions.

Pictures

The large gouache paintings displayed in this room were painted about 1794 by the Swiss artist Abraham-Louis-Rodolphe Ducros (1748–1810) for Sir John Acton. Several show activity in the Neapolitan dockyard at Castellammare, which Sir John did so much to modernise. Another depicts an elaborate picnic in a Chinoiserie pavilion in the woods near Castellammare. On the slopes above is the Casino Reale, which Acton used as his summer villa. The pictures are in their original matching frames.

On the left-hand wall is a watercolour by Raffaelle d'Aurea of *Marianne, Lady Acton* with her daughter Elizabeth and one of her sons, wearing fancy dress, on a terrace in Sicily.

On the north wall is a portrait of *Sir John Acton*.

The *miniatures and silhouettes* are late 18th- and early 19th-century.

Above **The Ante-Room**

Left *An Assembly in a Chinese Pavilion*; by A.-L.-R. Ducros

Sir John Acton (1736–1811), prime minister of Naples

Born in France and brought up as a Catholic, Acton made his name serving in the Tuscan navy. In 1778 he was appointed to reform the moribund Neapolitan navy, which he did with great energy, modernising the dockyard at Castellammare. By 1789 he had become *de facto* prime minister of Naples. Sir William Hamilton, the British ambassador in Naples, thought him to be 'still an Englishman at heart', and in 1798 Acton sided with England in its war against France. He was driven from power by a pro-French faction and eventually retired to Sicily.

In 1800, to general astonishment, he married his niece Marianne Acton: he was 63, she was only thirteen. Their daughter Elizabeth married Sir Robert Throckmorton, 8th Bt. Marianne came to live at Coughton after Elizabeth's marriage, bringing with her the pictures now on display in this room and many other treasures still at Coughton.

Furniture

The set of *early Georgian chairs* has interlaced splats on their backs. The *Georgian centre-table* has a brass-bound top made from a single slice of walnut.

The black *papier-mâché dressing-table set* is said to have been bought at the Great Exhibition of 1851. Papier mâché was a popular material for furniture at that time and is surprisingly strong.

The Tapestry Bedroom

Pictures

The portraits are largely of 18th-century Throckmortons and their relations. Particularly fine are the pastels by William Hoare of Bath of *Sir Robert Throckmorton, 4th Bt*, who is shown holding a drawing of the temple he had built at Buckland House in 1755–7, and of his daughter, *Barbara*, in a white feathered hat.

Furniture and textiles

The *Victorian bed* is known as a 'half-tester' from the small canopy. The *pillow lace* was embroidered by Mrs Kettle, who was the housekeeper at Coughton in 1844.

The walnut *wardrobe* is known as an *armoire* (meaning 'closed cupboard') and dates from the 1600s. It is Dutch or Flemish in origin, but the influence of the Far East, so popular at this time, can be seen in the carvings.

The *fragments of tapestry* were woven in Brussels in the 16th century.

Metalwork

The glass case at the foot of the bed displays *19th-century Venetian silver filigree work*.

Below The Tapestry Bedroom

The Tribune

This room embodies the Throckmorton family's journey from danger to triumph. Throughout the 1500s and 1600s, the Catholic relics that can be seen here would have been hidden away from public view. Their discovery would have put their owners' lives at certain risk. With Catholic Emancipation in 1829, the family were at last free to display their beliefs and their treasures openly, for all to see.

Katherine of Aragon's cope

The magnificent early 16th-century cope of purple velvet is embroidered in gold thread with the Virgin and Child, seraphim, pomegranates and flowers. This is said to have been the work of Henry VIII's first queen, the devoutly Catholic Katherine of Aragon, and her ladies-in-waiting. Conservation by the National Trust's textile workshop at Blickling Hall in 2001–4 has restored its glowing colours.

Right *The Nativity*; a 15th-century alabaster relief

Below right An English illuminated Book of Hours, *c.*1500

Picture

The portrait is of *Sir Nicholas Throckmorton* (1515–71), who – unusually for a Throckmorton – was a Protestant. He served Queen Elizabeth as her ambassador in France for many years (see p.33).

Sculpture

The 15th-century *carved relief* of Nottingham alabaster depicts the Nativity.

Manuscripts

In the glass case are several medieval illuminated religious books, including service books such as the Sarum Rite. All have been passed through the generations of the Throckmorton family. They include the oldest bindings to be found in the entire National Trust collection.

Mary, Queen of Scots' chemise

In the glass case to the right of the window is the linen chemise of 'the holy martyr, Mary, Queen of Scots' (according to the Latin inscription stitched on the front of it in red silk). After many years imprisonment, Mary was executed at Fotheringhay Castle in 1587. She is said to have worn the chemise on the day of her death. It was given to Sir Charles Throckmorton, 7th Bt, in 1820.

Above is a copy of the marble *effigy of Mary* that her son, James I, commissioned from Cornelius and William Cure for her tomb in Westminster Abbey.

The **panelling** is identical to that in the Dining Room next door and was put up here in 1827, when Sir Charles Throckmorton recorded in his diary: 'Began Oaking the Tribune.' It must have come from an enormous single room at Weston – possibly a long gallery.

Jacobite relics

After James II was deposed in 1688, many English Catholics (known as Jacobites) worked to return him or his descendants to the throne. In the glass case in this room are displayed a *glove* belonging to James III (the Old Pretender) and a *Garter ribbon* of his son, Prince Charles Edward Stuart (the Young Pretender).

The *broken sword* belonged to the 3rd Baronet, and before that to Captain John Smith. At the Battle of Edgehill in October 1642, Captain Smith crossed enemy lines under cover of darkness to rescue the seized Royal Standard. On returning it to the King, Captain Smith was knighted on the spot.

The Saloon
The Saloon Passage

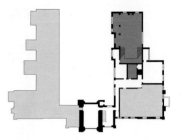

The Saloon

In the Tudor house this was the great hall, where the whole household would have gathered to eat or be entertained on special occasions. It served as a covert chapel between 1688, when the east wing was ransacked, and 1855, when the Catholic chapel in the park was completed. The family would have participated in services from the level of the Tribune, while the rest of the household worshipped below, the two spaces separated by three shuttered openings.

The shutters were replaced by the wooden panelling in 1910, when Sir William Throckmorton comprehensively remodelled the space to create the present Saloon. (His portrait hangs on the north wall.) He redeployed the Elizabethan double staircase from Harvington Hall, another family house near Kidderminster which has many priest's holes. For many years Harvington had been occupied by the family's Catholic chaplains, who would have used this staircase every day.

Today, this room is used for family celebrations and for public concerts and other entertainments in the weeks leading up to Christmas.

Pictures

The portraits are largely of 19th- and 20th-century Throckmortons. The large portrait to the right of the fireplace is of *Elizabeth Acton, Lady Throckmorton* with two of her children by John Partridge. Portraits of her father, *Sir John*

Above The Saloon

Acton (see p.21), and her brothers, *Richard* and *Cardinal Charles Acton*, hang nearby.

Other portraits include *Lt-Col. Courtenay Throckmorton*, who was painted posthumously after he had died in action in 1916. Next to him is a portrait of his granddaughter *Mrs Clare McLaren-Throckmorton*, who has lived at Coughton since 1992. The photographs include one of Sir Robert, the last Throckmorton baronet to live at Coughton, together with the writer Roald Dahl, who was married to his niece.

Furniture

The *Broadwood piano, c.*1909, displays family photographs, including one of Mrs McLaren-Throckmorton's father, Prof. Alphonsus d'Abreu, who was a pioneering heart surgeon at the Queen Elizabeth Hospital, Birmingham. The other pieces include a mid-17th-century *deed case*, a fine Regency *sofa* and two *Knole settees*.

Militaria

In the north-east corner (far left-hand side) of the room is a small case of military medals and the armband and sword-stick used by Col. Courtenay Throckmorton at the coronation of George V. The same case also contains the armband and sword-stick used by his younger brother Geoffrey at the coronation of George VI.

Lighting

The sumptuous *chandeliers* were made around 1870-1910 by Perry & Co. of Birmingham, who used circular double-cut drops of the highest quality.

The Saloon Passage

The glass case on your right as you leave the Saloon contains memorabilia of Mary Throckmorton, who served as lady-in-waiting to Elizabeth, Empress of Austria in Vienna (see p.43).

This passage was previously a wine cellar. Behind a panel you can see what may have been another priest's hole, which was discovered by Lilian, Lady Throckmorton in 1929.

Fixed to the panelling is a copy of Edward VIII's original Letter of Abdication, addressed to the House of Commons, where Geoffrey Throckmorton was at the time serving as Clerk of the Journals.

Made between sunrise and sunset

At the bottom of the left-hand stair is the famous *Throckmorton coat*. In 1811 Sir John Throckmorton wagered 1,000 guineas that his estate staff could shear two of his sheep, spin and weave the wool, and dye, cut and stitch the cloth to make a finished coat – all between sunrise and sunset. Sir John won the bet and is shown wearing the result in the portrait over the fireplace. The nearby poster and the painting on the north wall celebrate the achievement.

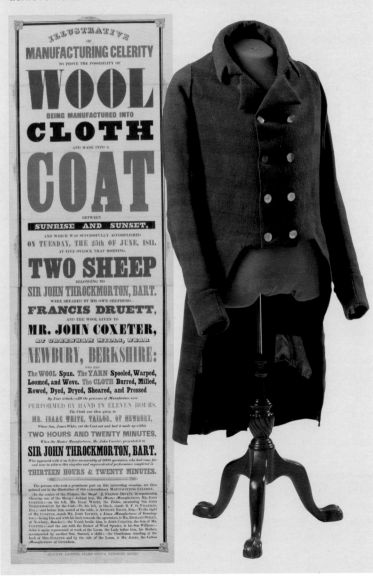

The Garden

Since 1991 the previously somewhat desolate garden has been transformed by Clare Throckmorton and her daughter Christina Williams, who won two gold medals at the 2010 RHS Chelsea Flower Show. Together, they continue to guide what has been one of the most ambitious garden revival projects in the Midlands. Their aim has been twofold: to create a garden worthy of such an important historic house; and to provide enjoyment for visitors. The emphasis throughout has been on variety, in planting and design, combining the best of old and new, and extending the flowering period so that there will always be something of interest for visitors, whatever the season. The successful completion of the new Walled Garden has shown what is possible, but it is only the start. There is much more to come, and every reason for return visits in future years.

The Central Courtyard

This was the first part of the garden to be tackled by Mrs Throckmorton, in the autumn of 1991. The new design focuses on a central fountain with a Bath stone rim designed by David Brain. He based its shape on the quatrefoils that decorate the little corner turrets of the Gatehouse. The fountain is surrounded by four box-edged island beds inspired by Elizabethan knot gardens. The spring planting here includes the tulips succeeded in early summer by roses. The fountain is aligned with the Gatehouse, but to maintain the appearance of symmetry in what is actually a very unsymmetrical space, the flower border against the north wing has been extended.

openings in it to the river, park and hills beyond. The ornamental trees include chestnuts, cherries, thorns and acers.

The West Front

In 1993 the dreary expanse of gravel was reduced and realigned to run parallel with the west front of Coughton. At the same time the grass was extended to produce a more welcoming setting for the entrance front. Six Portuguese laurels, clipped into pyramid shapes, flank the Gatehouse.

The Walled Garden

This occupies an L-shaped area of two acres adjoining St Peter's church. The new design was conceived by Mrs Throckmorton's daughter, Christina Williams, who trained at the English Gardening School in Chelsea. It comprises a series of linked 'garden rooms' in the tradition of Hidcote and Sissinghurst. The focus is on flowers, with a rose labyrinth, bower seats and wooden Gothic arches to support climbers. Stone steps, again designed by David Brain, lead down to a rectangular pond.

The new Walled Garden opened in 1996, and in 2006 received the World Federation of Rose Societies' Award of Garden Excellence – a first in the UK.

The Lime Tree Walks and Sunken Gardens

Extending in parallel from the north and south wings are two double lines of pollarded red-twigged limes. They were planted flanking the central lawn in 1992 by students from nearby Pershore College to provide shady walks.

Beyond the Lime Tree Walks lie two Sunken Gardens, which are planted with scented roses. A circular yew hedge forms a rotunda between them, enclosing the east side of the lawn, but also offering views through

The Bog Garden

Inspired by a water garden at Forde Abbey in Dorset, it was designed to make better use of a waterlogged part of the garden and to encourage wildlife.

The Riverside Walk

There is an attractive walk along the river Arrow, which has been extensively replanted since 1992 with *Narcissus* 'February Gold' and *actaea* and *Chionodoxa luciliae*. It also features over 100,000 daffodils propagated by an American member of the Throckmorton family.

Philip's Garden

This lies beyond the weir stream in an area which is densely shaded by alders and often flooded in winter. It is named after its creator, the Harrogate horticulturalist Philip Swindells, who has planted it with such water-loving plants as iris, primula, hellebore and fern.

St Peter's (Anglican) church

The church, which lies immediately to the south of Coughton Court, is largely Perpendicular in style, having been rebuilt by Sir Robert Throckmorton in the early 16th century at the same time as the house.

Above The Bog Garden

Opposite The Riverside Walk

Fragments of early stained glass survive in the windows. The south doorway was given a Gothick makeover in the 1780s, just like the house.

There is a particularly fine collection of Throckmorton monuments. The nave is dominated by a large table tomb, which was commissioned by Sir Robert, but never occupied by him, as he died on crusade in 1519. Another Sir Robert (the 4th Baronet) was buried in it in 1791. In the north chancel is a tomb chest bearing brasses of Sir George (d.1553) in armour and his wife Katherine. Below are figures of their eight sons and eleven daughters. In the south chancel are further substantial tombs commemorating Sir Robert (d.1570) and Sir John (d.1580), in his lawyer's robes with his wife Margery.

SS Peter, Paul and Elizabeth's (Catholic) church

When the Throckmortons were at last allowed to worship openly, they commissioned John Hansom to build this chapel in 1851. The spacious interior is aisleless and contains a fine alabaster reredos and east window by Hardman of Birmingham. The building is in need of restoration.

The Throckmortons of Coughton

The Throckmortons take their name from a little hamlet near Fladbury in Worcestershire, which lies in the shadow of Bredon Hill. Here they farmed land for the bishops of Worcester for centuries. They first became established at Coughton following the marriage in 1409 of John Throckmorton to Eleanor Spiney, who was heiress to part of the Coughton estate.

John Throckmorton was a lawyer, who served the powerful Beauchamp earls of Warwick. He also fought in France during the Agincourt campaign of 1415 and was Chamberlain of the Exchequer, an influential post at the court of Henry V. John reinforced his family's new status in the traditional way – by buying more land in Warwickshire and Worcestershire. At his death in 1445 he was buried in Fladbury church beneath a grand tomb, which still has its commemorative brass.

John's eldest son, Thomas Throckmorton (d.1472), followed a similar path, acquiring the rest of the Coughton estate in 1449 from the Tracy family and marrying well. His wife Margaret Olney brought with her the substantial Buckinghamshire estate of Weston Underwood, which was to become the family's favourite residence in the 17th century.

Sir Robert Throckmorton (c.1451–1519)

He consolidated the family's position in Warwickshire and established it in national politics. Having backed the winning side in the

The church of St Peter was rebuilt by Sir Robert Throckmorton in the early 16th century

Right The heraldic stained glass in the Blue Drawing Room celebrates 15th- and 16th-century Throckmorton marriages

Wars of the Roses, he fought for Henry VII at the battle of Stoke in 1487. He was knighted by a grateful monarch in 1494 at the same time as the king's son, the future Henry VIII, and was also appointed to the Privy Council. His marriage to Katherine Marrowe, the daughter of a London alderman, produced five sons and seven daughters.

Sir Robert needed a country house to match his position: it was he who probably began building the Coughton gatehouse and remodelled the church in the fashionable Perpendicular style. In his will he left money to erect a chantry chapel, where masses would be said for the salvation of his soul. (It was also to be used as a classroom for teaching the children of his tenants.) Sir Robert's elaborate canopied tomb dominates the nave of the church, but his body was buried far from home. He died in Rome in 1519 while on a pilgrimage to the Holy Land.

By a mixture of acquisitiveness, careful marriages and royal service, the Throckmortons had risen in three generations from the ranks of the minor gentry to the dangerous world of the Tudor court.

Sir George Throckmorton (c.1489–1552)

Catholic opponent of the Reformation

George trained as a lawyer and by 1512 had married Katherine Vaux, which brought him into the circle of the Parrs, the family of Henry VIII's sixth wife. By the 1520s he was serving in the royal household, where he showed a talent for making trouble. He fought a long legal battle with the King's chief minister Cardinal Wolsey over land near Coughton that he was keen to acquire. After much argument, the dispute was eventually settled amicably. He was knighted about 1526 and three years later was elected MP for Worcestershire in the Reformation Parliament.

Sir George remained a staunch Catholic and during the following decade was a leading member of the group that met at the Queen's Head tavern in London to resist the King's divorce and reformation of the church. After a particularly fiery speech in the Commons in 1532, Sir George was brought before the King and asked to explain why he opposed the King's planned marriage to Anne Boleyn. Sir George's reply was frank in the extreme: 'It is thought that ye have meddled with both the mother and the sister.' Taken aback, Henry could only respond feebly: 'Never with the mother.' The Lord Chancellor, Thomas Cromwell, then promptly stepped in to deny that the King had ever slept with Anne's sister.

After this embarrassing exchange, it is perhaps not surprising that Cromwell urged Throckmorton 'to stay at home and meddle little with politics'. Sir George seems to have taken Cromwell's advice. In September 1536 he wrote from Coughton apologising that he had not been present during the King's tour of the Midlands. He explained that he had 'lain in Buckinghamshire [at Weston Underwood] this year, for the greater part of my house here is taken down.' He is probably referring here to the building of the gatehouse and the south range.

Sir George showed open sympathy for the 1536 religious rebellion known as the Pilgrimage of Grace. He was arrested and only escaped execution by making a contrite apology to the King. Cromwell's fall in 1540 strengthened Throckmorton's position, enabling him to acquire Cromwell's nearby estate at Oversley in 1542. In all, he was to have eight sons and eleven daughters, who presented him with no fewer than 112 grandchildren.

Sir Robert Throckmorton (d.c.1580)

Persecuted for his faith

Sir George's eldest son was an equally steadfast Catholic, when this was a dangerous thing to be. He was probably responsible for creating the priest hole in the gatehouse at Coughton (see p.17). Another was discovered at Weston Underwood, which he remodelled about 1578. Three of his daughters were married to fellow Catholics: Mary to Edward Arderne; Anne to Sir William Catesby;

Left Katherine Vaux married Sir George Throckmorton by 1512

Right Sir Robert Throckmorton

Muriel to Sir Thomas Tresham, who built Lyveden New Bield in Northamptonshire, an extraordinary celebration of Catholicism in stone which is also now in the care of the National Trust. His niece, Bess, married Sir Walter Raleigh (see p.14).

Francis Throckmorton (1554–84)
Plotter

Sir Nicholas's cousin shared a weakness for plotting, but in the Catholic cause. He backed plans for a Spanish invasion that would have put the Catholic Mary, Queen of Scots on the throne in place of Elizabeth and restore the old religion. In 1583 Francis was arrested in possession of incriminating letters, and under torture, he eventually confessed. On 10 July 1584 he was executed at Tyburn, dying 'very stubbornly' and unrepentant.

Sir Nicholas Throckmorton (1515–71)
An undiplomatic diplomat

Not all Throckmortons were Catholics. Sir Robert's younger brother chose to practise the new religion, perhaps after having served in the evangelical Protestant household of his cousin, Catherine Parr. Her marriage to Henry VIII in 1543 brought Nicholas Throckmorton to court, where he prospered during the brief reign of the Protestant Edward VI: when he brought news of English victory at the battle of Pinkie, the young king promptly knighted him.

On Edward's death in 1553, Sir Nicholas tried to prevent his cousin Thomas Tresham from proclaiming the Catholic Mary Tudor as Queen, supporting instead the claim of the Protestant Lady Jane Grey. When this plan failed, he became involved in Sir Thomas Wyatt's rebellion against Queen Mary in 1554. He was sent to the Tower and put on trial for treason. Tudor treason trials usually had only one outcome, but, amazingly, Throckmorton managed to outwit the prosecution in court, and was acquitted. He fled to France and expected to be granted high office when Elizabeth became queen in 1558. However, he was outmanoeuvred by his rival, the Queen's chief minister, William Cecil, who forced him to remain in Paris as British ambassador. He showered Elizabeth with gifts, including jewellery, clocks and 'two pair of parfumed gloves', but to no avail. He ended his days in frustration and disappointment.

CONCILIVM SEPTEM NOBILIVM ANGLORVM CONIVRANTIVM IN NECEM IACOBI · I ·
MAGNÆ. BRITANNIÆ. REGIS TOTIVSQ· ANGLICI CONVOCATI PARLEMENTI ·

Bates — Robert Winter — Christopher Wright — Iohn Wright — Thomas Percy — Guido Fawkes — Robert Catesby — Thomas Winter

Opposite The priest's hole in the Tower Room provided a refuge for Catholic priests

Right The Gunpowder Plotters of 1605. Four of the conspirators were related to the Throckmortons

Thomas Throckmorton (1533–1614)

Recusant

Thomas inherited Coughton in 1581 and as one of the most prominent recusants in the Midlands endured fines and imprisonment during the harsh years of late Elizabethan persecution. In March 1593 – while Thomas was in jail and his sister Mary Arderne was temporarily mistress of Coughton – the house was searched by government 'witchfinders'. The report to the Privy Council noted:

> There was resistance offered at such time as you did search the house, and … they of the household there did not carry themselves with that dutiful course and obedience they ought to do, and … divers superstitious things and furniture for Mass was there found, and it was confessed that a priest being a seminary was harboured there at that time, who was conveyed out of the way and or lieth hid in some secret place.

Mrs Arderne was arrested and interrogated, together with 'the rest of her servants whom you shall think fit to be restrained'.

The Gunpowder Plot

Persecution of the kind suffered by the Throckmortons, perhaps inevitably, provoked retaliation. The most notorious instance was the Gunpowder Plot of 1605. The Throckmortons themselves were not involved, but four of the chief plotters were cousins, including Robert Catesby and Francis Tresham. Thomas Throckmorton was staying at Weston Underwood at the time, having rented Coughton to another of the conspirators, Sir Everard Digby, for 'hunting' (Digby's role was to kidnap the King's daughter, the nine-year-old Princess Elizabeth). On All Saints' Day (1 November 1605) Father Henry Garnet preached a sermon at Coughton on the text: 'Take away the perfidious people from the territory of the Faithful'. This was later taken as open support for the plotters, but in fact Garnet was simply voicing his concern at the persecution Catholics were suffering. When news reached Coughton of the plot on 6 November, he was appalled: 'We are all utterly undone'. His words proved accurate. The conspirators were quickly rounded up, and Garnet himself was executed on 3 May 1606.

Sⁱ ROBᵀ THROCKMORTON CREATED BARᵀ 1642
DIED 1650.
BURIED AT COUGHTON.

Above Sir Robert
Throckmorton, 1st Bt;
English School, 17th-
century

Sir Robert Throckmorton, 1st Bt (d.1650)

Thomas Throckmorton was succeeded by his grandson, Robert. As a 'confined recusant', he had to seek permission to leave Coughton in his early years. Under Charles I, conditions for Catholics like Robert Throckmorton were gradually relaxed to such an extent that he became a Royalist and was created a baronet by the King in 1642. However, the outbreak of the Civil War that year brought fresh turmoil to Coughton. In 1642 the house was occupied by a Parliamentary garrison, as one of the soldiers described:

We lay at a place called Cofton in Warwickshire, and there lived a great Papist, one Frogmorton, who hearing of our coming fled away from his house, and his whole Family, which the soldiers did plunder, and found abundance of Images and Pictures, which they broke and committed to the fire.

Further damage was done when Coughton was bombarded by a Royalist force. The Parliamentary garrison finally left in January 1644, but only after setting fire to the house in three places. A later report noted that 'the gate house [was] dismantled and the house quite ruined'. To make matters worse, the estate was confiscated by Parliament.

When Sir Robert died in 1650, the prospects for both Coughton and the Throckmortons looked bleak.

Sʳ FRANCIS THROCKMORTON BARᵗ
DIED 1680

Above **Sir Francis
Throckmorton, 2nd Bt;
School of Sir Peter Lely**

Sir Francis Throckmorton, 2nd Bt (1641–80)

Repairing Coughton

Sir Francis was only eight at his father's death, but while he was growing up, his trustees managed to recover the estate from Parliament. In 1659 he married Anne Monson to the sound of a fanfare of trumpets. He bought himself a wedding gown of Indian silk and an expensive new hat for the occasion. The couple lived mainly at Weston Underwood and at Moor Hall in Warwickshire, but gradually the devastated Coughton was made habitable once again. Between 1663 and 1665 £2,355 was spent on 100,000 red bricks and new stonework and roof-tiles for the Dutch gables.

Anne and Francis had four children, but at some point the marriage turned sour. Francis's traumatic childhood had made him melancholy and careful with money. Anne, in contrast, loved extravagance and playing cards. They separated and after an unhappy court battle she was granted an allowance of £350 and 'such access to her children as is fit for a mother at convenient times'; she also agreed 'to maintain her youngest daughter out of the said allowance'. Anne Throckmorton survived her estranged husband by almost 50 years, living on alone at Coughton until 1728.

Sir Robert Throckmorton, 3rd Bt (1662–1720)

Coughton ransacked once more

Sir Robert continued the process of restoring Coughton by forming a private Catholic chapel in the east wing. This was destroyed by a mob from Alcester on what became known as 'Running Thursday' – the anti-Catholic riots of 3 December 1688 that followed the overthrow of the Catholic James II. The east wing was to remain derelict for the next century. Sir Robert's additions of 1710 to Weston have fared rather better; indeed, one of his new wings is all that has survived of that house.

In 1690 Sir Robert married Mary Yate, who brought yet more property into the family – the estates of Harvington in Worcestershire and Buckland in Berkshire.

Sir Robert Throckmorton, 4th Bt (1702–91)

Making Coughton more Gothick

The 4th Baronet succeeded in 1720, when the family's fortunes were at their highest point and he was to enjoy spending that wealth over the next 71 years. By then the Throckmortons owned no fewer than four separate and substantial estates: Harvington, Weston, Buckland and Coughton. In his early years Sir Robert lived mostly at Weston, but from 1767 he made Buckland his principal residence, having commissioned John Wood the Younger to rebuild the house as a Palladian villa at vast expense. (He is said to have destroyed the bills out of shame at their size.) He surrounded the new house at Buckland with a picturesque

aunt, sister and cousin, who were all serving as nuns in the English Augustinian convent in Paris. Sir Robert was depicted as a flamboyant 17th-century knight in armour, and when he finally turned his attention to Coughton in 1780, he adopted a similarly antiquarianising approach. The house was by then in a very dilapidated state. He began by demolishing the remains of the long-derelict east wing, using the rubble to fill in the moat that once surrounded the house.

He then rebuilt either side of the gatehouse and inserted an elegant staircase on one side to improve communications between his newly fan-vaulted entrance hall and the upper floors. Sir Robert's Gothick additions showed a rare respect for the Tudor fabric so that it is now quite difficult to distinguish new work from old. And it was entirely characteristic of the man that, when he died at the age of 88 in 1791, he chose to be buried, not in a new tomb, but at Coughton in the empty Tudor tomb of an earlier Sir Robert, who had died abroad in 1519.

Above **Catherine Collingwood** was the 4th Baronet's second wife; by George Knapton

Opposite above **Sir Robert Throckmorton, 3rd Bt**; English School, late 17th-century

Opposite below **Sir Robert Throckmorton, 4th Bt**; by William Hoare of Bath

Right **Anne Throckmorton as Prioress of the English Augustinian convent in Paris**; by Nicolas de Largillière

landscape garden complete with grotto and rotunda. The poet Henry Pye celebrated the way Sir Robert had:

Clothed the declining slopes with pendant wood
And o'er the sedge-grown meadows poured the flood.

Sir Robert filled Buckland with Old Master paintings and new portrait commissions. During a visit to France in 1729 he sat for Nicolas de Largillière, who also painted his

'A wretched old house with a handsome gate of stone.'

Horace Walpole after a visit in 1758

Sir John Courtenay Throckmorton, 5th Bt (1753–1819)

Catholic emancipator

Sir Robert outlived his eldest son and grandson, and so the title and estates passed to his second grandson. Sir John Courtenay Throckmorton belonged to the generation that began the gradual removal of the restrictions that had for over two centuries prevented English Catholics from taking a full part in public life. He returned from his Grand Tour of Italy in 1778 (see box), the year that the first Catholic Relief Act was passed. The passing of the second Relief Act in 1791 enabled him to create a new Catholic chapel in the house. He seems to have made few other changes, as he lived here little: an inventory taken in 1792 reveals that the house was very sparsely furnished. In the same year he helped to form the Cisalpine Club, which argued that English Catholics living north of the Alps (hence the name) would only win further concessions from the Protestant establishment, if they pledged allegiance to the King and diluted the Pope's power to appoint English clergy (whilst still accepting his authority in matters of dogma). Not surprisingly, this caused bitter argument between Catholic laity and clergy.

Sir George Throckmorton, 6th Bt (1754–1826)

Unlike most of his fellow Catholics, Sir John had liberal political leanings, becoming part of the circle of Charles James Fox and the Prince of Wales, who came for breakfast at Coughton in September 1806. He died childless in 1819, and so was succeeded briefly as 6th Baronet by his brother George, a gout-plagued invalid who had lived most of his life at Weston.

Right Robert Throckmorton; by Pompeo Batoni, 1772

Below Sir John Courtenay Throckmorton, 5th Bt; attributed to Thomas Phillips

SIR JOHN THROCKMORTON BART
BORN AT WESTON COM: BUCKS, JULY 27
1753, DIED AT BUCKLAND, COM: BERKS
JAN 3, 1819, BURIED AT COUGHTON.

THROCKMORTON ESQ^R SON OF GEORGE THROCKMORTON UNDERWOOD COM: BUCKS. BORN 1750. DIED 1779.

On the Grand Tour

In the 18th century, gentlemen completed their education by visiting the historic cities of Italy, culminating in Rome. English Catholics had an additional reason for making the trip. John's elder brother, Robert, was in Rome in 1772 (*pictured*). John and his younger brother George followed two years later, where their behaviour provoked disapproving comment: 'They frequent low English company, because there is the favourite card table of their tutor, unless when he chooses to exhibit with Cups & Balls, or declaim against the Jesuits in the vile hole of an English Coffee House … The two young gentlemen appear to be very capable of improvement, & the elder (Mr Courtenay) to be a most agreeable character.'

A poet friend

The poet William Cowper was befriended by Sir John and his brother George and their wives Maria and Catherine, who offered him a home at Weston Lodge on the Weston Underwood estate in 1786–95. The Throckmortons supported Cowper through his recurring bouts of melancholy. Cowper found relief walking through the mid-18th-century Wilderness Garden at Weston, to which the Throckmortons gave him a key. It was here that he wrote 'On the death of Mrs Throckmorton's Bullfinch' and other poems.

SIR GEORGE THROCKMORTON BAR^T. BORN AT WESTON, COM: BUCKS SEPT^R. 15^T. 1754, DIED AT WESTON, 27 OF JULY 1826. BURIED AT WESTON.

Above Sir George Throckmorton, 6th Bt; style of George Romney

SIR CHARLES THROCKMORTON BAR.T BORN 1757,
DIED ... MBER 1840.

Left Sir Charles
Throckmorton, 7th
Bt; English School,
early 19th-century

Opposite top
Sir Robert
Throckmorton, 8th
Bt; marble bust

Opposite below
Sir Robert
Throckmorton, 8th
Bt; by Thomas Phillips

Sir Charles Throckmorton, 7th Bt (1757–1840)

By the time the 4th Baronet's youngest grandchild inherited in 1825 at the age of 67, the expansive 18th-century era was over. Sir Charles decided that radical measures were necessary. He handed over Buckland to his nephew and heir, demolished Weston, and in 1827 returned to Coughton. Sir Charles was welcomed back to the family's ancestral home by cheering tenants, who erected floral archways and banners proclaiming 'May happiness enter with you', 'Proceed and prosper' and 'Long live Sir Charles'. Sir Charles was a red-faced countryman, a lover of hunting and natural history, who was widely liked despite his short temper. He chose to be painted out in the park with his gun and dog. He appreciated the antiquity of Coughton, but his attempts to embellish it were less sensitive than his grandfather's. He covered the west front with a hard cement in order to unify the house's appearance.

SIR ROBT THROCKMORTON BART.
B. 1800
D. 1862.

Sir Robert Throckmorton, 8th Bt (1800–62)

A Catholic chapel for Coughton

With the passing of the Catholic Emancipation Act in 1829, Catholics were at last allowed to serve as MPs once again. Sir Robert was one of nine English Catholics to swear the Oath of Allegiance and take their seats in the House of Commons for the first time in 300 years. He was also responsible for building the Catholic chapel that stands at the end of the south drive.

In 1829 he married Elizabeth Acton, the daughter of Sir John Acton, the former prime minister of Naples (see p.21). Elizabeth's brother Charles (later a cardinal) officiated at the wedding, which seems to have been an exuberant affair: one guest downed no fewer than 23 glasses of champagne.

A breath of fresh air

The 8th Baronet's daughter Mary was sent to Vienna to work as governess to Archduchess Valerie, the infant daughter of Emperor Franz Joseph of Austria. Unfortunately, her English enthusiasm for fresh air was not appreciated. When Valerie caught pneumonia, the doctors blamed Mary for continually opening the windows, and she was sacked. However, she remained on good terms with the Archduchess for the rest of her life.

Sir Wm Throckmorton Bart.
B. 1838.
D. 1919.

Left Sir William
Throckmorton, 9th Bt;
British School

Below Sir William's trunks

2182

Sir Wm Throckmorton Ba.

Sir William Throckmorton, 9th Bt (1838–1919)

Extravagance and retrenchment

William's coming-of-age in 1859 was celebrated at Coughton with great festivities and the planting of a double avenue of elms in front of the house. He succeeded the following year – the first time that Coughton had passed straightforwardly from father to son for 140 years. The total Throckmorton estate stood at over 22,000 acres, and on the surface all seemed well. He enjoyed the life of a free-spending bachelor, devoting much of his time to his beloved racehorses. A member of the

Jockey Club, he won the Great Jubilee Stakes at Kempton with Avington in 1894 and accumulated the trophies now displayed in the Dining Room. But the agricultural depression of the 1870s forced him to retrench. Weston and part of the Coughton estate were sold, and the rest let out. Finally, he decided to sell Buckland as well, moving back into Coughton in 1908. Little had been done to the house since the 1830s, so he set about a comprehensive renovation, installing an old staircase and panelling from Harvington and creating the Saloon. He loved Coughton for its ancientness, and was annoyed to discover that an over-energetic local priest had exorcised the resident ghost, the Pink Lady, without his permission.

By then Sir William was in his 70s, and his heir (his brother Richard) was not much younger. To secure Coughton's long-term future, he turned to Richard's eldest son, Courtenay, who was invited to come and live at Coughton with a young wife, Lilian Langford-Brooke. Alas, all Sir William's plans were destroyed by the First World War. In April 1916 Courtenay was killed in action in Mesopotamia (modern-day Iraq), leaving a young widow, a seven-year-old son, Robert, and two daughters. By fateful coincidence, the stone Throckmorton coat of arms fell from the gatehouse on the day of his death.

Left Lt-Col Richard Courtney Throckmorton, who was killed fighting in Mesopotamia (modern-day Iraq) in 1916; by John St Helier Lander

Above The Saloon

Modern times

Coughton was put in trust for Robert, who did not come of age until 1929. His widowed mother sold a further part of the Coughton estate in 1934, when land prices were at their lowest, but was determined to hold on to the house and the core of the park. Having inherited money from her own family, Lady Throckmorton was able to keep up the old ways during the interwar years. Three liveried footmen were employed to bring meals all the way from the kitchen in the north wing to the dining room on the first floor of the south wing. During the Second World War, when Robert was away serving in the Fleet Air Arm, Lady Throckmorton retreated to the south wing with a reduced staff of three. The rest of the house was occupied, appropriately, by children from the Catholic Coombe Bank convent school. The north wing was also made ready for the staff of the Speaker of the House of Commons in case the country should be invaded.

Lady Throckmorton was a great favourite of James Lees-Milne, the National Trust's Historic Buildings Secretary. In March 1948 he 'had tea with that angelic Lady Throckmorton, who looked thinner and not too well. She is all alone in this house, and has a struggle to keep going and make both ends meet. She is a noble and splendid woman.' Two years earlier, she had arranged for the freehold of the house to be transferred to the National Trust, with a 300-year leaseback to the family.

After Lady Throckmorton's death in 1955, the house was rearranged and redecorated by Sir Robert Throckmorton's second wife, Lady Isabel, who had learnt much from the restoration of another ancient house, Haddon Hall, by her father, the 9th Duke of Rutland. She also received useful advice from the interior designer and maverick conservationist Rick Stewart-Jones on behalf of the National Trust.

On Sir Robert's death in 1989 the title passed to his cousin Sir Anthony Throckmorton, who lived in America. The title died with him in 1994, but the fortunes of Coughton were once again revitalised by one of the female members of the family. Sir Robert had two sisters. The elder, Elizabeth, married a well-known and greatly respected heart surgeon, Professor d'Abreu. They had three daughters, the eldest of whom, Clare, inherited the Coughton lease and the Molland estate as her grandmother Lady Lilian had

intended, having bought out Sir Anthony's life-interest.

A QC and specialist in European Law, Clare Tritton (her professional name) left the Bar to devote her time to the management of both estates when she moved to Coughton in the early 1990s with her second husband Andrew, taking the name Throckmorton as a reflection of the commitment that she made to her ancestral family home

'Mrs T', as she is affectionately known, did much to restore the interiors and fortunes of the house, inheriting from her grandmother, Lady Lilian, a determined dedication to care for Coughton and protect it for the future. Together with her daughter, Christina Williams, she created the magnificent gardens, including the award-winning Walled Garden.

In 2006 the National Trust began a 15-year management agreement to continue opening the house to visitors. The family continue to live in the North Wing and to manage the gardens as part of a close working partnership with the National Trust, thus maintaining an extraordinary family connection going back over 600 years.

Sharing stories

Children love to visit their grandparents. For me, coming to Coughton has always been incredibly special – not least because of the stories my grandmother has told me over the years about my family and their involvement in iconic moments of national history including, of course, the Gunpowder Plot. What child wouldn't have treasured memories of this place? From imagining hiding away in the priest holes, to climbing the spiral staircase to the top of the Tower and riding our bikes around the gardens. As I have grown older, there have been different experiences to enjoy – family Christmases in the Saloon, as well as my 21st birthday party, which included dinner in the Dining Room and a big party in the garden. I come here as often as I can – there is always something new to see.

Today, Coughton is still very much our family home and we hope that you will enjoy it as such. It is with the continued support of our visitors that we and the National Trust are able to continue looking after it and sharing the stories of this special place.

Magnus Birch (Mrs McLaren-Throckmorton's eldest grandson)

Above Mrs Clare McLaren-Throckmorton with her children and grandchildren